Empire of One

The Solopreneur's Blueprint to Building your Online Kingdom

Joe Forrest

Niche of One

Copyright © 2024 by Joe Forrest

All rights reserved.

No portion of this book may be reproduced in any form without written permission from the publisher or author, except as permitted by U.S. copyright law.

This publication is designed to provide accurate and authoritative information in regard to the subject matter covered. It is sold with the understanding that neither the author nor the publisher is engaged in rendering legal, investment, accounting or other professional services. While the publisher and author have used their best efforts in preparing this book, they make no representations or warranties with respect to the accuracy or completeness of the contents of this book and specifically disclaim any implied warranties of merchantability or fitness for a particular purpose. No warranty may be created or extended by sales representatives or written sales materials. The advice and strategies contained herein may not be suitable for your situation. You should consult with a professional when appropriate. Neither the publisher nor the author shall be liable for any loss of profit or any other commercial damages, including but not limited to special, incidental, consequential, personal, or other damages.

2nd edition, 2025 – Niche of One Publishing

Contents

Introduction: From Noise to Signal	1
1. Start Here	5
2. Why Medium Works	9
3. The Only Structure That Matters	12
4. The Newsletter That Doesn't Suck	15
5. Building Something That Lasts	19
6. Making Things People Actually Buy	23
7. Building Your Tribe (Without the Hype)	27
8. The Right Way to Do Affiliate Marketing	32
9. Making It All Work Together	36
10. What to Do When It Works	40
11. Keeping Your Money Straight	45
12. When Things Don't Work (And How to Fix Them)	51
13. The Mistakes That Kill Creator Businesses	59
14. Your First 90 Days	64
15. Building Your Empire of One	71
About the author	74

Introduction: From Noise to Signal

Here's what I learned the hard way: the internet doesn't need another guru promising you'll make six figures in six months.

What it needs is fewer creators making better things.

I got laid off from a Fortune 50 company in 2023. Six-figure salary, benefits, the whole corporate package—gone. I won't bore you with the sob story, but I will tell you this: getting fired was the best worst thing that happened to me.

Not because I "found my passion" or "discovered my purpose." That's bullshit. I found something simpler and more useful: **a way to make things people actually want, without burning out or selling my soul.**

The Problem Isn't What You Think

Everyone's talking about building empires, scaling to the moon, becoming the next big thing. But here's what nobody mentions: most creators are drowning in their own complexity.

They're building seventeen different income streams, chasing every platform, trying to be everything to everyone. They're busy, not productive. Moving, not progressing.

I tried that. Built complicated funnels, launched courses nobody asked for, spent more time on marketing than making. It was exhausting and, honestly, kind of gross.

What Actually Works

Simple things. Made well. Shared honestly.

That's it.

Not "simple" as in lazy or basic. Simple as in **clear, focused, and repeatable.** Simple like a well-made tool that does one job perfectly.

This isn't about minimalism for aesthetics—it's about minimalism for results. Do less to be more. Cut the noise to amplify the signal.

Who This Is For

This guide is for creators who:

- Want to build something real without the circus
- Are tired of guru promises and growth hacks
- Have something to say but don't know how to say it profitably
- Believe good work should speak for itself (but know it needs help being heard)
- Want to create on their own terms, at human scale

If you're looking for get-rich-quick schemes or "passive income" fantasies, this isn't for you. If you want to build a sustainable creative practice that pays your bills and respects your time, keep reading.

What We're Building

Not just an empire. A practice.

Not just a brand. A reputation.

Not just a movement. A quiet revolution where creators stop performing and start making things that matter.

The goal isn't to get famous or go viral. It's to build something **simple, repeatable, and unmistakably yours.**

Let's begin.

1
START HERE

Stop reading about writing. Start writing.

I know, I know. You bought this guide to learn how to build a creator business. But here's the thing: most people never start because they're too busy getting ready to start.

They research platforms. They design logos. They plan content calendars six months out. They do everything except the one thing that matters: **making something.**

The Only Three Things You Need

Forget the complicated systems. Here's what you actually need to start making money as a creator:

1. **Something to say** (your niche)

2. **Somewhere to say it** (your platform)

3. **Someone to say it to** (your people)

That's it. Not seventeen tools, not a perfect brand strategy, not a content calendar that would make a Fortune 500 CMO weep with joy.

Three things.

Finding Your Something

Everyone tells you to "find your passion." That's terrible advice. Passion doesn't pay bills. **Usefulness does.**

Instead, find your overlap: What do you know that others want to learn?

I use a simple exercise. Write down:

- 3 things you're genuinely interested in
- 3 things you're decent at
- 3 problems you've solved (even small ones)

Look for connections. I'm interested in writing, I'm decent at systems, and I've solved the problem of making complex things simple. That overlap became my niche.

Your niche doesn't have to be revolutionary. It just has to be **yours.**

Picking Your Platform

You don't need to be everywhere. You need to be somewhere consistently.

I recommend starting with one platform and doing it well. Here's my honest take on the main options:

Medium: Built-in audience, pays from day one, handles all the tech stuff. You write, they handle everything else. Simple.

Newsletter: Direct connection to your people, no algorithm games, you own the relationship. Harder to grow but more valuable long-term.

Personal blog: Complete control, full ownership, no platform risk. Also requires the most work and technical knowledge.

Pick one. Commit to it for six months minimum. Platforms are tools, not destinations. The goal is to make good work, not to game algorithms.

Finding Your People

Here's what nobody tells you about building an audience: **you don't find them, they find you.**

Your job isn't to chase people. It's to be consistently useful in one place so they can find you when they're ready.

Write for one person. Solve one problem. Be helpful. Be human. The right people will show up.

The First 30 Days

Week 1: Pick your platform. Set up the basics. Publish one thing.

Week 2: Publish another thing. Notice what happens (probably nothing—that's normal).

Week 3: Keep publishing. Engage with others in your space. Be generous with comments and shares.

Week 4: Look back at what you've made. What felt natural? What got response? Double down on that.

Don't overthink it. The best creator business is the one that actually exists.

Start Ugly

Your first posts will be bad. Your early products will be rough. Your brand will evolve.

That's not a bug. **It's a feature.**

Perfect is the enemy of done, and done is the enemy of never starting. You can't edit a blank page, and you can't improve what doesn't exist.

Ship something today. It doesn't have to be great. It just has to be real.

2
Why Medium Works

Medium gets a lot of hate from "real" creators.

They say it's not your platform, you don't own your audience, the algorithm is unpredictable.

They're right about all of that. I still recommend it for beginners.

The Truth About Starting

When you're starting out, your biggest enemy isn't platform risk.

It's never publishing anything at all.

I spent two years building the "perfect" WordPress blog. Custom theme, optimized everything, analytics tracking every click. Know how much money it made me? Zero dollars.

You know what made me money on day one? Publishing on Medium with their paywall turned on.

What Medium Actually Gives You

An audience that already exists. You don't have to build from zero. People are actively browsing, searching, reading. Your job is to write something worth finding.

No technical overhead. No hosting, no updates, no broken plugins at 2 AM. You write, they handle everything else.

Built-in monetization. Turn on the paywall, write something useful, get paid. It's not much at first, but it's something. And something beats nothing.

Real feedback. Comments, claps, highlights. You'll know immediately if your work resonates. That feedback loop is gold for a new creator.

How to Actually Make Money There

Forget the growth hacks. Here's what actually works:

Write for the big four topics: Health, relationships, money, personal development. Not because they're trendy, but because they solve real problems people will pay to understand.

Use your expertise differently. If you're a programmer, don't just write about code. Write "How Debugging Taught Me to Fix My Relationships" or "The Minimalist Developer's Guide to Financial Planning."

Be useful first, clever second. The stories that pay are the ones that help. Entertainment is nice, but solutions get shared.

Tag strategically. Use all five tags. Pick ones with active communities. But don't game the system. Write first, optimize second.

The Secret Ingredient

Consistency beats everything else.

I made more money writing 200 mediocre articles than trying to craft 10 perfect ones. Volume teaches you what good looks like. Perfect teaches you what paralysis feels like.

Publish something every week. Or every day if you can swing it. The algorithm rewards consistency, but more importantly, **consistency rewards you** with practice, feedback, and gradual improvement.

Medium's Real Value

Medium isn't where you build your empire. It's where you learn to write for an audience that doesn't know you yet.

It's training wheels for creators. And there's no shame in training wheels when you're learning to ride.

Use it to figure out your voice, test your ideas, and make some money while you learn. Then, when you're ready, take those skills somewhere you own.

But for now? Just write. Medium will handle the rest.

3
The Only Structure That Matters

Forget the seventeen-step formulas.

Here's what actually works:

Hook them fast. Your first sentence is everything. Make it personal, surprising, or useful. "Most blog posts die in obscurity" works better than "In today's digital landscape..."

Name the problem. What's broken? What's frustrating? What keeps people up at night? Get specific. Pain that's named is pain that's shared.

Show the stakes. Why does this matter? What happens if nothing changes? Make them feel the cost of staying stuck.

Offer the way out. Give them something actionable. Not theory, not inspiration—**actual steps they can take today.**

Send them somewhere. End with a clear next action. Subscribe, try this, think about that. Never end with "What do you think? Let me know in the comments!"

What People Actually Want

Stories, not abstractions. "I failed at this and here's what I learned" beats "Here are five principles for success" every single time.

Specifics, not generalities. "I made $347 in my first month" is more useful than "You can make good money doing this."

Process, not just outcomes. Show your work. Share the messy middle, not just the highlight reel.

Honesty, not performance. Admit when you're wrong, confused, or still figuring it out. Perfect people are boring. Real people are magnetic.

The Secret of Good Writing

Good writing serves the reader, not the writer.

Before you publish anything, ask yourself: "What does this do for them?" If the answer is "shows how smart I am" or "promotes my stuff," rewrite it.

If the answer is "helps them solve a real problem" or "saves them time and confusion," you're on the right track.

Inspiration Is Everywhere

That frustrating conversation you had? Write about it.

The mistake you made last week? Write about it.

The tool that saved you three hours? Write about it.

Your regular life is someone else's breakthrough. The thing that seems obvious to you is revolutionary to someone who hasn't learned it yet.

How to Never Run Out of Ideas

Keep a note on your phone called "Things That Annoyed Me Today." Half of them will be perfect blog posts.

Another note: "Things That Worked." The rest of your content lives there.

The best writing isn't pulled from thin air—it's pulled from real experience. Your job isn't to be original, it's to be **useful and honest about what you've actually lived through.**

Edit Like You Mean It

First draft: get the ideas out.

Second draft: make it clearer.

Third draft: make it shorter.

Cut the throat-clearing. Delete the disclaimers. Remove the words that don't earn their place.

Your reader's time is more valuable than your ego. Respect it.

Write something worth their time. They'll give you more of it.

4
The Newsletter That Doesn't Suck

I've written newsletters that took six hours to produce and got zero replies.

I've also written ones that took six minutes and generated actual business.

Guess which approach I recommend?

Why Most Newsletters Fail

They try too hard. Ten thousand words about everything and nothing. Industry roundups nobody asked for. "Thought leadership" that sounds like it was written by a committee.

Or they go the other direction: pure sales pitch disguised as content. "Here's a tip! Now buy my thing!"

Both approaches treat your subscribers like they're stupid. They're not.

What Actually Works

Curation, not creation.

Your job isn't to reinvent the wheel every week. It's to find the best wheels and show people where they are.

Here's my entire newsletter formula:

- **One thing I made** (link to my latest article, product, or idea)
- **One thing I found** (link to something useful someone else made)
- **One quick thought** (two sentences max about why these matter)

That's it. Takes me ten minutes to write. My open rates are over 40%.

The Power of Less

Most people think newsletters need to be novels. Wrong.

Your subscribers are busy. They don't want to read War and Peace in their inbox every Tuesday. They want:

- **Something useful they can scan in 30 – 60 seconds**
- **Clear value without having to work for it**
- **Links that are actually worth clicking**

Less content, more curation. Less explanation, more recommendation.

How to Pick What to Share

My stuff: Whatever I published that week. If I didn't publish anything, I share something older that's relevant again. The goal is to remind people I exist and make useful things.

Other people's stuff: Things that made me think, tools that saved me time, articles that solved problems I'm having. I'm genuinely recommending things I found valuable.

The connecting thread: What do these two things have in common? Why are they both worth your subscriber's time? Make that connection explicit.

Subject Lines That Work

Forget the clickbait. Use clear, descriptive subject lines that tell people exactly what they're getting:

- "Two tools that saved me 3 hours this week"
- "Why I'm wrong about newsletters (+ a better approach)"
- "Quick find: the best writing app I've tried"

Boring? Maybe. But my subscribers know what they're getting, and they open emails because they want what's inside.

The Email That Builds Trust

Every newsletter should answer one question: "Why should I keep subscribing?"

Not with words, but with **consistent value delivered simply.**

When someone opens your email, they should immediately see something useful. When they click your links, they should find exactly what you promised.

Do that every week for six months, and you'll have real subscribers, not just numbers on a dashboard.

Tools That Don't Get in the Way

Use whatever email platform makes sense for your budget, but pick something simple. I use a self-hosted Ghost because it handles the technical stuff without requiring a PhD in email marketing. Plus, it also serves as my website/blog.

The tool doesn't matter. **Consistency does.**

Better to send a simple, useful email every week than to spend three months building the perfect newsletter system that you never actually use.

Start Small, Stay Useful

Your first newsletter might go to five people. Send it anyway.

Write like you're helping a friend, not building a media empire. The friend approach scales. The empire approach burns you out.

Good newsletters feel personal even when they go to thousands of people. Bad newsletters feel automated even when they go to five.

Be the good kind.

5

BUILDING SOMETHING THAT LASTS

Your brand isn't your logo.

It's not your color scheme or your carefully crafted mission statement.

Your brand is what people expect when they see your name.

That's it. Everything else is decoration.

What People Actually Remember

They remember how your work made them feel. Whether you delivered what you promised. If you showed up consistently or disappeared for three months without explanation. (Trust me on that last one.)

They remember if you were helpful or just hunting for attention. If your advice actually worked or if it was just recycled motivation.

They don't remember your tagline. They remember if they can trust you.

The Only Brand Strategy You Need

Be consistently useful as yourself.

Not as the person you think the market wants. Not as some polished version of yourself that tweets inspirational quotes and never admits uncertainty.

As the actual human being who solves real problems in your specific way.

I'm not trying to be the world's greatest writing teacher. I'm trying to be the clearest voice for creators who want to build simple, profitable things without losing their minds.

That's specific enough to be useful, broad enough to grow into, and honest enough to sustain.

What Consistency Really Means

It's not posting every day at 9 AM. It's not having perfect brand colors across seventeen platforms.

Consistency is being recognizably you in everything you make. Same values, same approach, same voice. Whether someone finds you through a tweet, a blog post, or a product description, they should think, "Yeah, this sounds like the same person."

Your writing voice should sound like you. Your products should solve problems the way you'd solve them. Your recommendations should reflect what you actually use and believe in.

Building Recognition, Not Fame

Fame is about getting attention. Recognition is about being remembered when someone needs what you offer.

You don't need everyone to know your name. You need the right people to think of you at the right time.

When someone in your space has a problem you solve, do they think of you? When they're recommending tools or resources, does your name come up?

That's recognition. It's smaller than fame but infinitely more valuable.

Your Values Are Your Filter

Every decision becomes easier when you know what you stand for:

- Do I take this collaboration? (Does it align with my values?)
- Do I write about this topic? (Does it serve my people?)
- Do I launch this product? (Would I actually use this myself?)

I value simplicity, honesty, and human-scale creation. So I don't promote complicated systems, I don't make promises I can't keep, and I don't push people toward burnout culture.

Your values aren't marketing copy. They're decision-making tools.

The Long Game

Building something that lasts means optimizing for years, not months.

That means saying no to opportunities that pay now but confuse your message. It means building relationships instead of just chasing metrics. It means creating things that will still be useful to someone in two years.

It means being patient with growth and impatient with lack of quality.

What People Actually Want

They want someone they can trust to cut through the noise and point them toward what actually works.

They want consistent quality, not constant volume. They want useful information delivered without drama or hype.

They want to feel like they're learning from a person, not being sold to by a machine.

Be that person. Everything else will follow.

Start Where You Are

You don't need a perfect brand strategy before you can begin building something people remember.

You just need to be consistently helpful as yourself. The rest develops naturally as you figure out what works and what doesn't.

Your brand isn't built in a boardroom. It's built one interaction at a time, one piece of work at a time, one person at a time.

Show up. Be useful. Stay human. Repeat.

6
Making Things People Actually Buy

I've launched products that took six months to build and sold three copies.

I've also made things in an afternoon that generated thousands in revenue.

The difference wasn't quality, marketing budget, or luck. **It was whether I built something people actually wanted.**

The Mistake Everyone Makes

We build what we think is cool instead of what solves real problems.

We spend months perfecting a course about "mindset mastery" when our audience is asking for a simple template to organize their ideas. We create comprehensive guides when people just want a quick checklist.

The market doesn't care how clever you are. It cares how useful you are.

What Actually Sells

Things that save time, reduce confusion, or solve immediate problems.

Not transformation. Not inspiration. **Practical solutions to specific frustrations.**

Your audience is telling you what they need. Listen to their questions:

- "How do I organize my newsletter ideas?"
- "What's the fastest way to write a product description?"
- "Which email platform should I actually use?"

Those questions are product opportunities hiding in plain sight.

The Simplest Products Win

Templates. The newsletter format that works. The blog post outline that gets engagement. The email sequence that converts.

Checklists. What to do before launching. How to set up your platform. Steps for writing your first paid article.

Guides. Not courses—guides. "Here's exactly how I do this specific thing, step by step."

Tools. Spreadsheets, Notion templates, simple calculators. Things that automate the annoying parts.

These aren't glamorous. They don't require months of development. **But they solve real problems for real money.**

How to Know What to Build

Ask your audience directly: "What's your biggest frustration with [topic]?"

Then build the smallest possible thing that addresses that frustration.

Not a comprehensive solution. Not the ultimate guide. **The smallest viable fix.**

A one-page checklist often outsells a 200-page course because it's exactly what someone needs right now.

The MVP Approach

Minimum Viable Product: The simplest version that delivers value.

Instead of building a complete course on productivity, create a single worksheet that helps people prioritize their daily tasks.

Instead of writing a book about business strategy, make a template for planning your first product launch.

Start small. Prove demand. Then expand if people want more.

Pricing That Makes Sense

Price based on value delivered, not time invested.

A template that saves someone three hours is worth more than a course that took you three weeks to create.

Start with what feels slightly uncomfortable. If you're not a little nervous about your price, it's probably too low.

Cheap signals worthless. Fair signals valuable.

Where to Sell

Start simple. Use platforms that handle payments, delivery, and support so you can focus on making good products.

Gumroad, Kit Commerce, even a simple PayPal link. The tool doesn't matter as much as actually selling something.

Perfect platforms don't make sales. Useful products do.

The Product That Sells Itself

The best marketing is a product that works exactly as promised.

When someone buys your template and it actually saves them time, they tell people. When your checklist prevents them from making expensive mistakes, they recommend it.

Make something so useful that customers become salespeople.

Start Today

What question did someone ask you this week? What problem do you see people struggling with repeatedly?

Build the smallest thing that helps with that. Price it fairly. Put it up for sale.

You can't improve a product that doesn't exist. You can't get feedback on something you never ship.

Make something small. Sell it to someone. Learn from what happens.

That's how real businesses start.

7
Building Your Tribe (Without the Hype)

Community building has become another hustle.

Everyone's launching Discord servers, hosting virtual summits, and promising to "build movements." Most of these communities die within six months because they were built for growth metrics, not genuine connection.

Real community happens when people help each other, not when they perform for you.

What Community Actually Is

It's not about having thousands of followers. It's about having people who show up consistently because they get value from being there.

It's not about engagement rates. It's about real humans solving real problems together.

Community is people choosing to spend their time with you and each other because that time feels well-spent.

The Foundation That Matters

Start with shared values, not shared interests.

Interests change. Someone might love productivity apps this month and hate them next month. But someone who values doing meaningful work without burning out? That's deeper.

I don't build community around "writing." I build it around **creating simple, useful things without losing your sanity.** That attracts people who think like I do about work, life, and what success actually looks like.

Small Groups Win

Ten engaged people beat a thousand lurkers.

I'd rather have a group where everyone knows each other's names than a massive audience where I'm shouting into the void.

Scale intimacy, not numbers. Make it feel personal even as it grows.

Where to Start

Your newsletter replies. When someone emails you back, that's community. Engage with them like they're a real person, not a metric.

Social media conversations. When someone comments thoughtfully on your work, respond thoughtfully back. Build relationships one interaction at a time.

Direct outreach. When you find someone doing interesting work in your space, reach out. Not to network—to genuinely connect.

Community isn't a platform. It's a practice.

What Keeps People Around

Consistency. Show up regularly. Not necessarily daily, but predictably. People can't join something that doesn't reliably exist.

Usefulness. Every interaction should leave someone better off than before. Share resources, make connections, solve problems.

Authenticity. Admit when you don't know something. Share failures alongside wins. Be human, not a highlight reel.

Clear boundaries. What's this community for? What behavior isn't okay? Clear expectations create psychological safety.

The Content That Builds Community

Behind-the-scenes process. "Here's how I'm thinking through this problem." People love seeing the messy middle.

Work in progress. "I'm building this thing—what am I missing?" Asking for input makes people feel invested.

Resource sharing. "This tool saved me three hours." "This article changed how I think about X." Be genuinely helpful.

Real stories. Not case studies—actual experiences. What worked, what didn't, what you learned.

Avoiding the Performance Trap

Don't try to be the motivational speaker. Be the person who shows up consistently with useful information and genuine interest in others.

Don't manufacture drama or urgency. Build trust through reliability and competence.

Don't try to be everyone's guru. Try to be someone's useful colleague.

When to Say No

Community building can become a full-time job if you let it. Set boundaries:

- You don't need to respond to every comment immediately
- You don't need to be available 24/7
- You don't need to solve everyone's problems
- You don't need to moderate every discussion

Your job is to create the space and set the tone. The community builds itself.

The Long View

Real community compounds over time. The people who stick around for two years become your best advocates, collaborators, and friends.

They're not there for the content—they're there for the connection. They trust your judgment, value your perspective, and want to see you succeed.

That's not something you can hack or growth-hack your way into. It's something you earn through consistent value and genuine care.

Start Small, Stay Real

Begin with the people already paying attention to your work. Engage with them like humans, not audiences.

Be helpful without expecting anything back. Share credit. Make connections between people.

Community isn't built—it's cultivated. Plant seeds, tend the soil, and trust the process.

8
The Right Way to Do Affiliate Marketing

Affiliate marketing has a reputation problem.

Most people think of sleazy "make money online" schemes, fake product reviews, and that one guy on Twitter who promotes seventeen different courses per week.

Done right, affiliate marketing is just honest recommendation with upside.

What Affiliate Marketing Actually Is

You recommend something you actually use. Someone buys it through your link. You get a small commission.

That's it. Not complicated, not unethical, not some get-rich-quick scheme.

It's word-of-mouth marketing with a paper trail.

The Only Rule That Matters

Only promote things you genuinely use and would recommend even without the commission.

If you wouldn't tell your best friend to buy it, don't promote it to your audience. Your reputation is worth more than any affiliate payout.

I've turned down affiliate deals worth thousands because the product didn't align with what I actually believe works.

What to Promote

Tools that solve real problems. The email platform you actually use. The writing app that changed your workflow. The course that legitimately helped you learn something valuable.

Products from people you respect. Creators whose work you follow, whose approach aligns with yours, whose success you're genuinely excited about.

Things that fit your audience. If you write about minimalism, don't promote productivity apps with seventeen features. Stay consistent with your values.

How to Recommend Without Being Gross

Tell the real story. How did you find this tool? What problem did it solve? What are the downsides?

Be specific about value. "This saved me three hours per week" is better than "This will change your life."

Disclose clearly. "I use ConvertKit for my newsletter and get a commission if you sign up through my link." Simple, honest, transparent.

Make it optional. Your content should be valuable whether someone clicks your affiliate link or not.

The Products That Actually Convert

Platforms and tools people are already considering. Email platforms, design tools, hosting services. People are going to buy something—help them choose well.

Educational products from credible creators. Courses, books, guides from people with proven track records.

Things with free trials or money-back guarantees. Lower risk for your audience, higher conversion for you.

Building Affiliate Relationships

Start with what you're already using. Most tools have affiliate programs. Apply for the ones you genuinely recommend.

Connect with creators you respect. If someone's course helped you, reach out. Not with a pitch—with gratitude and a question about partnership.

Be patient. The best affiliate relationships develop over time as you prove you can drive quality traffic and sales.

What Not to Do

Don't promote everything. If you're constantly selling, people stop trusting your recommendations.

Don't lie about usage. If you haven't actually tried something, don't pretend you have.

Don't hide the fact that it's an affiliate link. Transparency builds trust. Deception destroys it.

Don't make affiliate income your primary strategy. It should support your business, not be your business.

The Long-Term Approach

Build trust first, monetize second. Spend months providing value before asking for anything.

Recommend selectively. One great recommendation per month beats ten mediocre ones per week.

Track what works. Which products do your people actually buy? Focus on those.

Maintain relationships. The best affiliate programs come with ongoing support, exclusive access, and higher commission rates.

Making It Work on Platforms

In newsletters: Include one affiliate recommendation alongside your own content. Make it relevant to what you're sharing.

In blog posts: Natural mentions within helpful content work better than dedicated "review" posts.

On social media: Share genuine experiences with tools, with clear disclosure.

The Revenue Reality

Affiliate marketing won't make you rich overnight. My affiliate income started at $23 the first month and grew slowly from there.

But it's reliable supplemental income that compounds over time. As your audience grows and trusts you more, affiliate revenue grows too.

The Real Win

The best part isn't the money—it's the relationships.

When you promote someone's product thoughtfully, you're not just earning a commission. You're building a connection with another creator, helping your audience solve real problems, and strengthening your reputation as someone who gives good recommendations.

That's worth more than any commission check.

9
Making It All Work Together

You've got the pieces now.

A writing practice, a platform, some products, maybe a small community forming.

The question is: How do they connect? How does someone discover your work, trust you enough to subscribe, and eventually buy something?

This isn't about building a funnel. It's about creating a coherent experience.

The Journey That Actually Happens

Someone finds your article about productivity. It's useful, so they check out your other work. They see you have a newsletter and subscribe because they want more of that usefulness.

Over time, they notice you mention tools you actually use. Maybe they try one through your affiliate link. It works, so they trust your judgment more.

Eventually, they have a problem your product solves. They buy it because they already know you deliver value.

No tricks, no manipulation. Just consistent usefulness building trust over time.

How to Connect the Dots

Make your newsletter easy to find. Every blog post should mention it naturally. Not with a popup that covers the content—with a simple line that explains what subscribers get.

Cross-pollinate content. Your newsletter can expand on blog post ideas. Your blog posts can dive deeper into newsletter topics. Don't just repurpose—add layers.

Mention your products when relevant. If you write about email marketing, mention your email template naturally. Don't force it, but don't hide it either.

Share your process openly. When you use a tool or take a course, write about the experience. Some of those become affiliate recommendations.

The Ecosystem Approach

Think of everything as supporting everything else:

Your writing demonstrates your thinking and builds trust.

Your newsletter maintains connection between posts and creates a direct line to your audience.

Your products solve specific problems for people who already trust you.

Your affiliate recommendations help people while generating income that supports your writing.

Your community provides feedback that improves everything else.

Creating Natural Transitions

From reader to subscriber: Offer something immediately useful in exchange for an email address. Not a lead magnet—actual value.

From subscriber to customer: Solve small problems for free consistently. When they have a bigger problem, they'll consider your paid solution.

From customer to advocate: Deliver more value than promised. Make your customers feel smart for choosing you.

The Content Calendar That Works

Monday: Newsletter with your latest work + one useful thing you found.

Wednesday: Blog post solving a specific problem.

Friday: Social media sharing others' work and engaging with your community.

Simple rhythm. No overwhelm. Sustainable long-term.

Avoiding the Complexity Trap

The more pieces you add, the more chances for things to break down. Keep asking:

- Does this serve my audience or just my ego?
- Am I building systems or creating busywork?
- Would this still work if I simplified it by half?

Complexity is the enemy of consistency. Consistency is the engine of growth.

When Things Don't Connect

If people read your content but don't subscribe, your newsletter value proposition isn't clear enough.

If they subscribe but don't engage, your emails aren't useful enough.

If they engage but don't buy, you're not solving problems worth paying for.

Each disconnect tells you where to focus next.

The Patience Factor

This approach takes longer than growth hacks or viral strategies. But it builds something real.

Month 1: You're writing for yourself.Month 3: A few people are paying attention.Month 6: You have regular readers and some income.Month 12: You have a sustainable creative business.

It's not fast. But it works. And it lasts.

The Real Synergy

When everything works together, the whole becomes bigger than the sum of its parts.

Your writing gets better because you're solving real problems for real people. Your products improve because you understand your audience deeply. Your recommendations carry weight because people trust your judgment.

You're not just building an audience—you're building a reputation.

And reputation, once earned, becomes the foundation for everything else you want to create.

What to Do When It Works

You're making money now.

Not life-changing money, but real money. Your newsletter is growing. People are buying your products. You've got something that works.

Now what?

This is where most creators make their biggest mistake: they try to scale everything at once.

The Reinvestment Trap

When money starts coming in, the temptation is to spend it all on growth. Better tools, fancy courses, premium software, paid advertising.

Most of that spending is waste disguised as investment.

The best reinvestment is often in doing what's already working, but better.

What Actually Deserves Your Money

Time-savers, not time-wasters. Tools that automate the boring parts so you can focus on creating. Email scheduling, payment processing, simple analytics.

Education that fills specific gaps. Not random courses—targeted learning that solves problems you're actually facing.

Professional services for things you hate. Bookkeeping, basic design work, technical setup. Buy back your time for the work only you can do.

A financial buffer. Keep enough money aside to cover three months of expenses. Freelancer income fluctuates. Peace of mind is worth more than growth.

The Scaling Question

Before you expand, ask: **What's actually broken?**

If your problem is too few subscribers, focus on better content, not better tools. If your problem is low engagement, fix your newsletter, don't add new platforms.

Scale what works. Fix what's broken. Ignore everything else.

When to Say No

Success brings opportunities. Speaking gigs, collaboration requests, partnership offers. Most of them are distractions disguised as progress.

Say no to anything that:

- Doesn't align with your core message
- Requires skills you don't want to develop
- Takes you away from your main work for weeks
- Feels like it's just for the ego boost

Your attention is your most valuable asset. Protect it ruthlessly.

Growing Without Breaking

Add one thing at a time. If you want to start a podcast, don't also launch a course and join three new platforms. Pick one, do it well, then consider what's next.

Test before you invest. Before building a premium community, try a simple email group. Before creating a course, sell a worksheet. Validate demand with minimal effort.

Maintain what works. Don't let success in one area kill your fundamentals. Keep writing, keep showing up, keep being useful.

The Money Mindset

Save before you spend. Put aside money for taxes, business expenses, and personal emergencies before buying anything new.

Invest in assets, not expenses. A good website that lasts three years beats a fancy tool subscription you'll cancel in six months.

Track what matters. Revenue growth, subscriber quality, customer satisfaction. Not vanity metrics like social media followers or website traffic.

Building Systems, Not Dependencies

Document your processes. How do you write a newsletter? What's your product launch checklist? Write it down so it's repeatable.

Create templates. Email sequences, social media posts, product descriptions. Make it easy to maintain quality without starting from scratch each time.

Build multiple income streams. Don't depend entirely on one platform, one product, or one income source. Diversify thoughtfully.

The Success Tax

As you grow, expect new problems:

- Customer service takes more time
- Technical issues become more expensive
- Tax situations get more complicated
- People expect more from you

Plan for these costs. They're the price of success, not signs you're doing something wrong.

Staying Human at Scale

The bigger you get, the more tempting it becomes to automate everything and optimize for efficiency over authenticity.

Resist that. The human connection is what built your business. Don't sacrifice it for scale.

Keep writing your own emails. Respond to comments personally when you can. Remember that real people are choosing to spend their time and money with you.

The Long Game

Sustainable beats explosive. Building something that works for years is better than building something that works for months.

Quality compounds. Every great piece of work you create builds your reputation and makes the next piece easier to share.

Relationships matter more than metrics. The creators who last are the ones who build genuine connections, not just large audiences.

What Success Actually Looks Like

It's not the big house or the viral post or the feature in a major publication.

It's waking up excited about your work. It's solving problems you care about for people you respect. It's having enough money to live well without compromising what you believe in.

That's the real win. Everything else is just decoration.

KEEPING YOUR MONEY STRAIGHT

Nobody starts a creator business because they love bookkeeping.

But ignoring the money side will kill your creativity faster than any algorithm change. When you're stressed about taxes, confused about expenses, or surprised by fees, it's impossible to focus on making good work.

Handle the boring stuff so you can focus on the interesting stuff.

Separate Your Money

Open a business checking account. Even if you're just starting out, even if you're only making $50 a month. Keep business money separate from personal money.

This isn't just good practice—it makes taxes infinitely easier and helps you understand whether your business is actually profitable.

Use business accounts for business expenses. Domain name, email platform, design tools, courses that help your business. Everything goes through the business account.

Pay yourself from business to personal. Once a month, transfer your "salary" from business to personal.

This helps you see how much the business is actually making.

Track Your Income Sources

Keep a simple spreadsheet with columns for:

- Date
- Amount
- Source (Medium, affiliate, product sales, etc.)
- Platform fees
- Net amount

You need to know where your money comes from. Not just for taxes, but to understand what's working and what isn't.

If affiliate income is growing but product sales are flat, that tells you something about your audience and what they value.

Understand Your Real Costs

Platform fees: Medium takes a cut. Gumroad takes 10%. Most newsletter providers charge monthly. PayPal takes transaction fees.

Business expenses: Domain, hosting, email platform, design tools, education, equipment.

Taxes: Set aside 25-30% of your net income for taxes. Open a separate savings account just for this.

Your time: If you're spending 20 hours a week and making $200 a month, you're making $2.50 an hour. That's fine when you're learning, but not sustainable long-term.

Simple Pricing Psychology

Price testing: Start with what feels slightly uncomfortable. If you're not a little nervous about your price, it's probably too low.

Value-based pricing: A template that saves someone 3 hours is worth more than $5, regardless of how long it took you to make.

Bundle psychology: $47 feels much cheaper than $50. $97 feels much cheaper than $100. Use this.

Anchor pricing: If you have three products, price them at $19, $47, and $97. Most people will buy the middle option.

Tax Basics for Creators

Keep receipts for business expenses: Software subscriptions, equipment, courses that improve your skills, home office expenses if you work from home.

Track mileage: Trips to coworking spaces, meetups, conferences. Use an app like MileIQ.

Quarterly estimated taxes: If you're making more than $1,000 profit per year, you'll probably need to pay quarterly. Don't wait until April.

Consider an LLC: Once you're making consistent income, an LLC provides legal protection and can simplify taxes. Consult an accountant.

Banking and Payment Setup

Business checking: Local credit union or online bank. Avoid big banks with high fees.

Payment processing: Start with PayPal or Stripe. Add more options as you grow.

Invoicing: If you do any freelance work, use something simple like Wave or Invoice Ninja.

Savings: Keep 3-6 months of business expenses in a separate savings account. Creator income fluctuates.

What to Track

Monthly recurring revenue (MRR): Newsletter subscriptions, memberships, anything that repeats.

One-time sales: Products, courses, services.

Expenses: Keep it simple—just track the total amount going out each month.

Profit: Income minus expenses. This is what actually matters.

Time invested: Rough estimate of hours worked. Helps you understand your real hourly rate.

Red Flags to Watch For

Spending more than you make: Common in the first few months, dangerous after that.

No money set aside for taxes: April will be painful if you haven't planned for this.

Too many subscriptions: Review monthly subscriptions quarterly. Cancel what you're not actively using.

No emergency fund: One bad month shouldn't kill your business.

Tools That Actually Help

Accounting: Wave (free), QuickBooks (overkill for most creators), or just a well-organized spreadsheet.

Banking: Any credit union or online bank with low fees.

Tax prep: TurboTax or similar if your situation is simple. CPA if you're making serious money.

Expense tracking: Your bank's app plus a spreadsheet. Don't overcomplicate it.

When to Get Help

Hire an accountant when:

- You're making more than $50k/year
- You have employees or contractors
- Your tax situation gets complicated
- You're spending more time on bookkeeping than creating

Hire a bookkeeper when:

- You're successful enough that your time is worth more than $20/hour
- You hate dealing with financial stuff
- You're making mistakes that cost money

The Real Goal

Financial clarity gives you creative freedom.

When you know exactly how much you're making, what you're spending, and what you owe in taxes, you can make better decisions about everything else.

You can confidently invest in tools that will help. You can price your products appropriately. You can plan for growth without panicking about cash flow.

Handle the money basics so you can focus on the work that matters.

When Things Don't Work (And How to Fix Them)

Everything breaks eventually.

Your email open rates tank. Your latest post gets zero engagement. You run out of things to write about. Sales stop.

This isn't failure. It's feedback. **The difference between creators who succeed and those who quit is how they respond when things stop working.**

Here's your troubleshooting guide for the most common problems.

Problem: Nobody Opens Your Emails

Symptoms: Open rates below 20%, declining subscriber engagement, lots of unsubscribes.

Likely causes:

- Boring subject lines that don't promise value
- Inconsistent sending schedule
- Too much selling, not enough helping
- Your content doesn't match what people signed up for

Fixes:

- Write subject lines that tell people exactly what they'll get: "3 tools that saved me 4 hours this week"

- Send on the same day/time every week

- Follow the 80/20 rule: 80% value, 20% promotion

- Survey your subscribers: "What do you want to learn about?"

- Test sending at different times

Quick test: Send a "What do you want?" email asking subscribers what they're struggling with. If that doesn't get replies, your list might be dead.

Problem: Your Posts Get No Engagement

Symptoms: No comments, shares, or meaningful interaction despite decent view numbers.

Likely causes:

- Writing about topics instead of problems

- Not asking for engagement

- Posting at bad times

- Your audience doesn't know you want interaction

Fixes:

- End posts with specific questions, not "What do you think?"

- Write about mistakes you've made and lessons learned

- Share work in progress and ask for feedback

- Respond to every comment like it's from a friend

- Post when your audience is actually online

Quick test: Write a vulnerable post about something you're struggling with. Real problems get real responses.

Problem: You've Run Out of Content Ideas

Symptoms: Staring at blank pages, recycling old topics, feeling like you have nothing new to say.

Likely causes:

- Not documenting your daily experiences
- Trying to be original instead of useful
- Not engaging with your audience's questions
- Consuming too little, creating too much

Fixes:

- Keep an "ideas" note on your phone. Add to it daily
- Answer questions from your audience directly
- Write about tools you use, mistakes you make, lessons you learn
- Curate and comment on other people's work
- Take breaks to learn new things

Idea starters:

- "Here's what I learned this week"
- "This tool saved me [X hours]"
- "I was wrong about [topic]"
- "How I [specific process]"

- "Why [common advice] doesn't work"

Problem: No One's Buying Your Products

Symptoms: Lots of traffic, decent email list, but no sales.

Likely causes:

- Solving problems people don't have
- Pricing too high or too low for your audience
- Not enough trust built before asking for money
- Unclear value proposition

Fixes:

- Ask your audience what they're willing to pay to solve
- Start with smaller, cheaper products to build trust
- Share customer results and testimonials
- Make your value proposition clearer: "This saves you X hours" or "This helps you achieve Y"
- Create urgency with limited-time offers

Quick test: Offer a free consultation or audit to 5 people. What problems do they actually want to pay to solve?

Problem: Your Growth Has Stalled

Symptoms: Subscriber growth is flat, revenue isn't increasing, feels like you're spinning your wheels.

Likely causes:

- Audience is too broad or too narrow

- Not enough distribution channels
- Content quality has plateaued
- Not reinvesting in growth

Fixes:

- Double down on what's working instead of adding new platforms
- Guest post or collaborate with other creators
- Improve your best content and reshare it
- Invest in better tools or education
- Ask successful customers to refer others

Quick test: Analyze your top 5 pieces of content. What do they have in common? Make more like those.

Problem: You're Burning Out

Symptoms: Dreading content creation, working constantly, feeling overwhelmed by your business.

Likely causes:

- No boundaries between work and life
- Trying to do everything yourself
- Comparing yourself to others constantly
- Working in your business instead of on it

Fixes:

- Set specific work hours and stick to them
- Batch similar tasks together

- Hire help for things you hate doing
- Take actual days off
- Focus on systems that reduce daily decisions

Emergency protocol: Take a week off. The world won't end. Come back with perspective.

Problem: Imposter Syndrome is Crushing You

Symptoms: Feeling like a fraud, afraid to charge money, convinced you don't know enough to help anyone.

Likely causes:

- Comparing your beginning to someone else's middle
- Waiting for permission that will never come
- Focusing on what you don't know instead of what you do

Fixes:

- Remember that you only need to be one step ahead of the people you're helping
- Document your learning journey publicly
- Collect testimonials and positive feedback
- Focus on serving others instead of proving yourself

Reality check: If your advice has helped even one person, you're qualified to help others.

Problem: You're Not Making Enough Money

Symptoms: Working hard but barely covering expenses, can't quit your day job.

Likely causes:

- Products priced too low
- Not enough products or income streams
- Audience too small for current pricing
- Not optimizing for revenue

Fixes:

- Raise your prices (seriously, try doubling them)
- Create higher-priced offerings for your best customers
- Focus on recurring revenue (subscriptions, memberships)
- Analyze what's actually profitable and do more of that
- Cut expenses that don't drive growth

Quick test: Email your best customers asking what premium product they'd pay $200+ for.

The Meta-Solution

Most problems have the same root cause: **you've stopped listening to your audience.**

When things aren't working:

1. Ask your audience what they need

2. Look at your analytics for clues

3. Test small changes before big pivots

4. Get feedback from actual customers, not just other creators

Fix the relationship with your audience, and most other problems solve themselves.

When to Pivot vs. When to Persist

Pivot when:

- You've tried multiple fixes over 3+ months with no improvement
- Your audience clearly wants something different than what you're offering
- You're consistently miserable doing the work

Persist when:

- You're seeing slow but steady growth
- Your audience is engaged even if it's small
- You believe in what you're building

Remember: Most overnight successes took years of consistent effort. Don't mistake patience for failure.

The Mistakes That Kill Creator Businesses

I've made every mistake in this chapter.

Some of them multiple times.

These aren't small tactical errors. They're the big strategic mistakes that can derail months or years of work. The kind that make you question whether this whole creator thing is actually possible.

The good news: they're all avoidable once you know what to watch for.

Mistake #1: Copying Someone Else's Strategy

You see a creator making $10K a month with YouTube videos, so you start making YouTube videos. Never mind that you hate being on camera and your audience prefers written content.

Or you try to replicate someone's launch strategy without understanding why it worked for them, their audience, or their specific situation.

Your audience isn't their audience. Your strengths aren't their strengths. Your life isn't their life.

What works: Study principles, not tactics. Learn why something worked, then adapt it to your situation, strengths, and audience.

Mistake #2: Building for an Imaginary Future Audience

You create content for the audience you want instead of the audience you have.

Writing advanced strategy pieces when your current readers need basic how-to guides. Building premium products when people are still figuring out if they trust you with free content.

Serve the people who are actually paying attention to you right now.

What works: Look at your analytics, read your comments, pay attention to the questions you get. Build for the people who are already there.

Mistake #3: Starting Too Many Things at Once

The "diversification" trap. You launch a podcast, start a YouTube channel, begin selling courses, and open a membership community all in the same month.

Six weeks later, nothing is working well and you're exhausted.

Focus is your competitive advantage. Most creators are scattered. Be the one who goes deep instead of wide.

What works: Pick one thing and do it consistently for six months minimum. Then, maybe, consider adding something else.

Mistake #4: Perfectionism Disguised as Strategy

Spending three months "researching" email platforms instead of sending emails. Building the perfect website instead of writing content. Planning the ultimate course instead of creating a simple worksheet.

Preparation becomes procrastination when it prevents you from shipping.

What works: Set deadlines for decisions. "I'll pick an email platform by Friday and send my first newsletter next Monday." Then stick to it.

Mistake #5: Chasing Every Shiny Object

New platform launches, and you have to be there. Someone mentions a growth hack, and you drop everything to try it. You hear about a monetization strategy and pivot your entire business model.

Consistency beats optimization. Better to do one thing well for a year than to try twelve things for a month each.

What works: Write down your current strategy. When you're tempted by something new, ask: "Will this make my current strategy work better, or am I just bored?"

Mistake #6: Underpricing Out of Fear

You price your products at what you'd pay, not what they're worth. Or you're so afraid of seeming "salesy" that you practically give everything away.

Cheap doesn't build trust—it signals desperation.

What works: Price based on value delivered, not your comfort level. If your template saves someone three hours, it's worth more than $5.

Mistake #7: Ignoring Your Business Basics

You're making money but have no idea where it's going. No separate business account, no tax planning, no understanding of your actual profit margins.

Financial chaos kills creativity. It's hard to focus on making good work when you're stressed about money.

What works: Set up simple systems early. Separate accounts, basic bookkeeping, money set aside for taxes. Boring but essential.

Mistake #8: Building on Rented Land Only

Putting all your energy into platforms you don't control. Building your entire audience on one social media platform, or relying completely on one income source.

Diversification isn't about having seventeen revenue streams—it's about not having all your eggs in one basket.

What works: Own your audience (email list), own your content (your website), own your products (not just affiliate income).

Mistake #9: Burning Out for Growth

Working seven days a week, responding to every comment immediately, saying yes to every opportunity. Treating your creator business like a startup that needs to scale or die.

Sustainable beats explosive. The creators who last are the ones who build businesses that don't require them to work 80-hour weeks.

What works: Set boundaries. Take days off. Remember that consistency over years beats intensity over months.

Mistake #10: Giving Up Too Early

Expecting results in weeks instead of months. Quitting when the initial excitement wears off but before the compound effects kick in.

Most creator businesses take 6-12 months to generate meaningful income. That's not failure—that's normal.

What works: Set realistic expectations. Track small wins. Focus on process metrics (posts published, emails sent) rather than just outcome metrics (money made, followers gained).

The Meta-Mistake

All of these mistakes have one thing in common: **they're based on fear instead of value.**

Fear of not growing fast enough. Fear of not being taken seriously. Fear of missing out. Fear of not being good enough.

Focus on being useful instead of being perfect, and most of these mistakes become impossible to make.

The creators who succeed long-term aren't the ones who avoid all mistakes—they're the ones who make mistakes quickly, learn from them, and keep shipping.

Your First 90 Days

Starting is the hardest part.

Not because the work is difficult, but because you have infinite options and no data about what works for you yet.

This 90-day plan removes the guesswork. Follow it exactly, and you'll have a functioning creator business by the end. Not a perfect one—a real one.

The goal isn't to get rich in 90 days. It's to build the foundation for everything that comes next.

Days 1-7: Setup Week

Day 1: Pick your three passion areas. Write them down. This is your niche of one.

Day 2: Choose your platform. Medium if you want to start earning immediately. Newsletter if you want to own your audience. Blog if you want complete control. Pick one.

Day 3: Set up your accounts. Platform account, email platform (No money? Use Substack. Want to own your platform? Use Ghost.), simple analytics.

Day 4: Write your first piece. 500-800 words about a problem you've solved. Publish it.

Day 5: Set up your money systems. Business checking account, simple expense tracking, tax savings account.

Day 6: Create your first lead magnet. Simple checklist, template, or guide related to your niche. Nothing fancy.

Day 7: Plan your content calendar. What will you write about for the next month? Brainstorm 10 topics.

Days 8-30: Consistency Phase

Week 2:

- Publish 2 pieces of content
- Send your first newsletter (even if you have 3 subscribers)
- Engage with 5 other creators in your space daily
- Document what you're learning

Week 3:

- Publish 2 pieces of content
- Send newsletter #2
- Start building your first simple product (template, checklist, guide)
- Join relevant communities and be helpful

Week 4:

- Publish 2 pieces of content
- Send newsletter #3
- Finish your first product
- Set up payment processing (Gumroad, PayPal, Stripe)

Daily habits:

- Write for 30 minutes minimum
- Engage authentically with your audience
- Track your metrics (subscribers, views, engagement)
- Save receipts and track expenses

Days 31-60: Validation Phase

Week 5-6:

- Launch your first paid product ($5-25 range)
- Write about your experience creating it
- Ask your audience what they're struggling with
- Experiment with different content formats

Week 7-8:

- Analyze what's working (check your metrics)
- Double down on your best-performing content types
- Start building your second product based on audience feedback
- Consider one affiliate partnership with a tool you actually use

Goals for this phase:

- Make your first $1 online
- Get 50+ email subscribers
- Understand which topics resonate most

- Build a consistent publishing rhythm

Days 61-90: Growth Phase

Week 9-10:

- Launch product #2
- Guest post or collaborate with one other creator
- Optimize your best-performing content
- Start building social proof (testimonials, case studies)

Week 11-12:

- Evaluate what's working and what isn't
- Plan your content strategy for the next 90 days
- Consider expanding to one additional platform (but only if current platform is working)
- Set up more robust systems for growth

Week 13:

- Celebrate your progress
- Write about what you've learned
- Plan your next product based on 90 days of audience interaction
- Set goals for days 91-180

Weekly Minimums

Content: 1-2 pieces per week, every week. Consistency beats perfection.

Newsletter: Once per week minimum. Same day each week.

Engagement: Respond to comments, engage with other creators, be part of the community.

Metrics review: Check your numbers weekly. What's growing? What's not?

Success Metrics for 90 Days

Realistic goals:

- 100+ email subscribers
- $100+ in revenue (products + affiliates)
- 20+ published pieces of content
- Clear understanding of your audience's biggest problems

Stretch goals:

- 300+ email subscribers
- $500+ in revenue
- One product that's selling consistently
- Guest appearance or collaboration completed

Common 90-Day Pitfalls

Week 2-3: The excitement wears off. Push through anyway.

Week 6-8: Comparing yourself to creators who've been at this for years. Focus on your own progress.

Week 10-12: Wanting to pivot or add new platforms. Resist the urge unless something is clearly broken.

Throughout: Perfectionism. Ship messy work rather than perfect work that never gets finished.

What to Do When You Hit Walls

No one's reading your stuff: Focus on solving specific problems, not general topics.

No email signups: Make your lead magnet more valuable or easier to find.

No sales: You might be selling to the wrong audience or solving the wrong problem.

Feeling overwhelmed: Simplify. Cut back to the bare minimum and focus on consistency.

After 90 Days

You'll have:

- A publishing habit that's sustainable
- Data about what your audience actually wants
- Multiple income streams (even if they're small)
- Systems that can scale as you grow
- Confidence that this actually works

Most importantly, you'll have momentum. The hardest part of building a creator business is proving to yourself that it's possible.

After 90 days of consistent work, you'll know it's possible because you'll have done it.

The Real Secret

This plan works not because it's perfect, but because it's **simple enough to actually follow.**

Most people fail not because they pick the wrong strategy, but because they pick a strategy they can't sustain.

90 days of imperfect consistency beats 30 days of perfect execution followed by giving up.

Start today. Follow the plan. Adjust as needed, but don't quit.

Your creator business is 90 days away.

15

BUILDING YOUR EMPIRE OF ONE

We've covered the mechanics.

Platforms, products, newsletters, community. But here's what really matters: **you already have everything you need to start.**

Not perfect tools, not a flawless strategy, not complete clarity about your future. You have experiences, perspectives, and problems you've solved that someone else needs to learn about.

The world doesn't need another guru. It needs more people sharing what actually works.

What You've Learned

How to start simple and build systematically. How to write with your real voice instead of copying someone else's formula. How to create products people want instead of products you think are clever.

How to build community without hype, recommend things without being sleazy, and make money without losing your soul.

But mostly, you've learned that sustainable creator businesses are built on consistency, not inspiration.

The Path Forward

Start where you are. Pick one platform and show up there regularly. Write about problems you've actually faced and solutions that actually work.

Be useful before you're clever. Be human before you're professional. Be consistent before you're perfect.

Ship something this week. Not because it's ready, but because shipping teaches you what ready actually looks like.

What Changes

You'll get better at seeing what people need. You'll develop instincts for what resonates and what falls flat. You'll build confidence in your own perspective.

You'll stop comparing yourself to creators with different goals, different audiences, different definitions of success.

You'll become unmistakably yourself in a marketplace full of people trying to be someone else.

What Doesn't Change

The fundamentals. Show up consistently. Solve real problems. Deliver what you promise. Treat your audience like humans, not metrics.

Stay curious about your craft. Keep learning, but don't let learning become a substitute for doing.

Remember that sustainable success comes from building trust over time, not from viral moments or growth hacks.

Your Niche of One

It's not about finding a tiny market and dominating it. It's about being the only person who approaches your topics in your specific way.

The only person who combines your particular interests, experiences, and perspectives. The only person who solves problems the way you solve them.

That's not a limitation—it's your competitive advantage.

The Work Begins Now

Close this guide. Open a blank document. Write about something that frustrated you this week and how you handled it.

Publish it somewhere. See what happens.

Then do it again next week.

That's how every successful creator business starts: one useful piece of work, shared with one real person, repeated until it becomes something bigger.

The internet needs fewer empires and more authentic voices. Fewer gurus and more people willing to share what they've learned.

Be one of those people.

Your empire is waiting.

About the Author

Who I Am (And Why I Write)

I'm Joe Forrest.

USAF Veteran. Husband. Dad. Grandfather. Creator. Storyteller. Someone who's been knocked down more than a few times and still chooses to stand back up.

I served during Operation Enduring Freedom and Operation Iraqi Freedom. That time left its mark – physically, mentally, spiritually. After the military, I spent years managing big projects at companies like GoDaddy, Google, and CBRE. The titles were nice, but they were never the point.

What's always been at the center for me is this:**Stories.**

Telling them.
Living them.
Using them to make sense of a messy world.

I got laid off from a Fortune 50 company in 2023. Six-figure salary, benefits, the whole corporate package – gone. Getting fired was the best worst thing that happened to me.

Not because I "found my passion" or "discovered my purpose." That's bullshit.

I found something simpler and more useful: **a way to make things people actually want, without burning out or selling my soul.**

What I Believe

I believe in doing meaningful work, slowly if needed, sustainably if possible, and **publicly if helpful.**

I don't believe in gurus, get-rich-quick schemes, or building empires on the backs of burned-out creators.

I value simplicity, honesty, and human-scale creation. So I don't promote complicated systems, I don't make promises I can't keep, and I don't push people toward burnout culture.

Your values aren't marketing copy. They're decision-making tools.

My Work

Now, I write for people who've been through it.People building from scratch.People who want to create things with integrity, intention, and grit.

My work is about turning experience into something useful. Something that might help someone else make it through.

Niche of One

I run a newsletter called **Niche of One**. It's built for creators who don't have a big team or a big budget—just a desire to build something real.

If you're into DIY minimalist creation, streamlined strategy, and honest talk about the ups and downs of making things...You'll probably feel right at home.

Subscribe to the newsletter
Read on Substack
Find my books on Amazon

www.ingramcontent.com/pod-product-compliance
Lightning Source LLC
Chambersburg PA
CBHW070357230526
45471CB00006B/2605